Creating
DECORATIVE CHAIRS
for Children

Sammie Crawford

4880 Lower Valley Road • Atglen, PA 19310

3 0645 14092710

Designed by RoS
Type set in Minion Pro/Swis721 Lt BT

ISBN: 978-0-7643-4854-9

Printed in China

Other Schiffer Books by the Author:

Building Gourd Birdhouses with the Fairy Gourdmother
ISBN 978-0-76433-7369

Creating Gourd Birds with the Fairy Gourdmother
ISBN 978-0-7643-335-2

Gourd Fun for Everyone
ISBN 978-0-7643-3124-4

Published by Schiffer Publishing, Ltd.
4880 Lower Valley Road
Atglen, PA 19310
Phone: (610) 593-1777; Fax: (610) 593-2002
E-mail: Info@schifferbooks.com

For our complete selection of fine books on this and related subjects, please visit our website at www.schifferbooks.com. You may also write for a free catalog.

This book may be purchased from the publisher. Please try your bookstore first.

We are always looking for people to write books on new and related subjects. If you have an idea for a book, please contact us at proposals@schifferbooks.com.

Schiffer Publishing's titles are available at special discounts for bulk purchases for sales promotions or premiums. Special editions, including personalized covers, corporate imprints, and excerpts can be created in large quantities for special needs. For more information, contact the publisher.

Dedication

This book is dedicated to the two friends who started me down this road, Gail Ezelle and Richard Bingham. Thanks to their requests to paint their chairs, I was inspired to keep going after I finished them.

Acknowledgment

Thanks again to my wonderfully talented husband. He made silk purses out of some of the ugliest sow's ears you can imagine. Without his help, I could not have done this book.

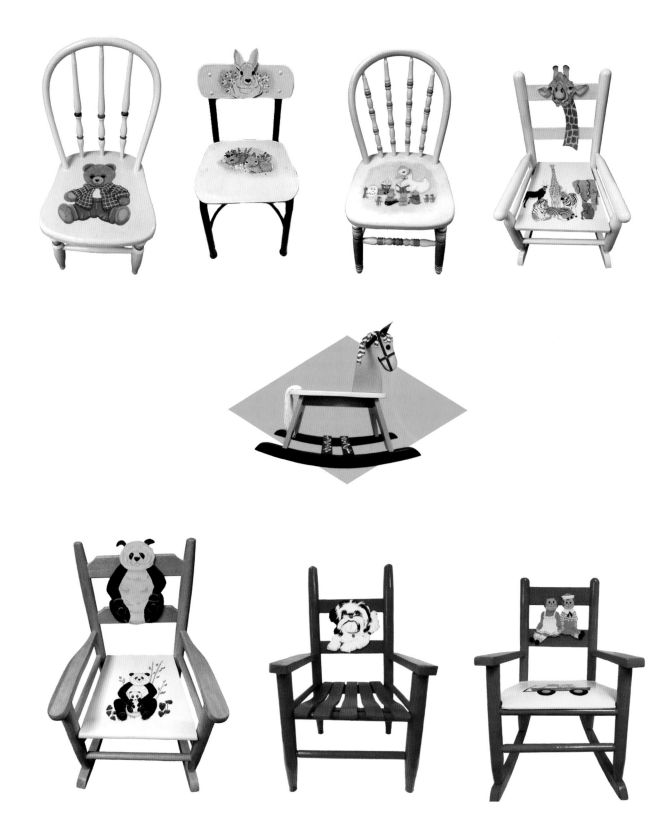

CONTENTS

INTRODUCTION

The chair painting idea was sparked by a friend who asked my husband to repair a child's chair that had been in the family for generations. When he finished restoring it, he painted it white. It looked like a blank canvas to me, and I couldn't stand the idea of not putting something on that white seat. When the friend's girlfriend saw the chair I had painted, she said "I have one, too. Would you mind painting something on it?" Well, you don't have to ask me twice to paint, and the journey began. On one of my searches, I met a little lady who was ninety-five years old. A rocker she received for her fifth birthday was for sale. Until then, I hadn't paid more than $10 for a chair to paint, but I was glad to part with $20 because of its story, and I felt I could add another fifty or sixty years to its life. I suspect it won't be long before I'm back to painting gourds, but this has been an enjoyable departure.

Supplies:

You should have on hand the standard supplies for transferring the patterns and painting the chairs:

- Tracing paper
- Transfer paper
- Stylus
- White and gray chalk pencils
- Q-tips or cotton swabs
- Paper towels
- Palette paper
- Blending gel
- Spray varnish
- Staple gun
- Assorted brushes

Transferring Patterns:

To transfer a pattern onto a piece for painting, first trace the pattern onto pattern paper. This is like thin tissue paper. Then position the pattern where you want it on the piece. Holding it in place with one hand, slip a sheet of transfer paper between the pattern and the piece. Use your stylus to trace over the lines. Before you begin tracing, be sure the transfer paper's correct side is down. If I had a nickel for every pattern I've traced only to discover the transfer paper was upside down, I'd be living next door to Donald Trump!

If using new transfer paper, whether black or white, turn it over and lightly rub with a paper towel. This will remove excess transfer and keep your piece cleaner. Even if it does get excess transfer on it, don't worry. It can be removed with a damp Q-tip or paper towel. If all else fails, just paint over it.

Palette—DecoArt
- Admiral Blue
- Asphaltum
- Black
- Black Plum
- Burnt Umber
- Camel
- Deep Midnight
- Emperor's Gold
- French Grey Blue
- Raw Sienna
- Sable
- Tuscan Red
- White
- Williamsburg Blue
- Winter Blue

Brushes—Loew-Cornell
- Series 7300 #12 flat
- Series 7350 10/0 liner
- Series 7520 ½" filbert rake

Supplies
- Thrift store chair
- Gloss spray varnish
- White enamel spray paint

Preparation
1. Make any needed repairs and spray paint the chair white.

Painting the Design
1. Apply the pattern and basecoat the bear with Sable.

2. Shade with Burnt Umber and use the rake brush and Camel to pull hair all over the bear. Also use this color to highlight.

3. The muzzle and pads are Camel with Asphaltum stitches.

4. Float Raw Sienna around the muzzle and inside the ears.

5. The nose, mouth, and eyes are Black with a White float across the tops of the eyes and the nose.

Bear Chair

6. Place a White comma stroke in each eye.

7. The jeans are a 2:1 mix of Williamsburg Blue & Admiral Blue.

8. Shade with a 3:2 mix of French Grey Blue and Deep Midnight.

9. Highlight with Winter Blue.

10. The buttons are Emperor's Gold.

11. The shirt is Tuscan Red shaded with Black Plum.

12. Use the liner brush and White for the lines.

Finishing
Finish with several light coats of spray varnish.

Palette—DecoArt
- Antique Mauve
- Black
- Bleached Sand
- Driftwood
- French Mauve
- Hauser Dk. Green
- Hauser Lt. Green
- Hauser Med. Green
- Lavender
- Mint Julep
- Ms. Mud
- Mustard Seed
- Pink Chiffon
- Raw Umber
- Shading Flesh
- Slate Grey
- Soft Lilac
- Spice Pink
- Violet Haze
- White
- Wild Orchid
- Wisteria

Brushes—Loew-Cornell
- Series 7000 #6 round
- Series 7300 #12 flat
- Series 7350 10/0 liner
- Series 7520 ½" filbert rake
- #275 ½" mop

Supplies
- Blending gel
- ¼" Masonite®
- Craft saw
- Sandpaper
- Thrift store chair
- White enamel spray paint
- Gloss spray varnish

Big Bunny

1. Apply blending gel to the back of the chair.

2. Tap in Soft Lilac and mop to soften and blend.

3. The bunny is White.

4. Use the filbert rake to shade with Slate Grey.

5. Wash with White if it appears too stark.

6. The eyes and nose are Black.

7. Float Pink Chiffon inside the ears.

8. Float White in the eyes and across the nose, and add White comma strokes in each eye.

9. Paint the daisies like those on the seat.

10. Paint the curlicues and leaves Hauser Med. Green.

Finishing
Finish with several light coats of spray varnish.

1

2

3

Palette—DecoArt

- Base Flesh
- Black
- Black Plum
- Bluegrass
- Butterscotch
- Cashmere Beige
- Cinnamon Drop
- Cocoa
- Country Blue
- Deep Teal
- Dioxazine Purple
- French Vanilla
- Georgia Clay
- Grey Sky
- Hauser Med. Green
- Heritage Brick
- Hi-lite Flesh
- Jade
- Lt. Avocado
- Lt. Buttermilk
- Mistletoe
- Moon Yellow
- Napa Red
- Neutral Grey
- Primary Yellow
- Russet
- Sapphire Blue
- Sand
- Shading Flesh
- Slate Grey
- Spiced Pumpkin
- Taffy Cream
- Terra Cotta
- Traditional Raw Sienna
- True Ochre
- Violet Haze
- White
- Winter Blue
- Wisteria

Brushes—Loew-Cornell

- Series 7300 #12 flat
- Series 7350 10/0 liner
- Series 7500 #3 round
- Series 7550 1" wash
- #275 1" mop

Preparation

1. Make any needed repairs and spray the chair white.

Painting the Design

1. Apply blending gel and use a 1:1 mix of Winter Blue and White to sponge an area on the seat a little larger than the pattern.

2. When dry, apply the pattern. Shade around all the characters with Winter Blue.

3. Paint the legs and spindles Country Blue, Mistletoe, and French Vanilla.

4. **Goose:** Basecoat White and shade with Grey Sky.

5. Her bonnet and beak are Moon Yellow shaded with True Ochre and highlighted with Sand.

6. The ribbon is Country Blue shaded with Sapphire Blue and highlighted with Winter Blue.

7. Paint the eye Black and add a White float.

Supplies

- Thrift store child's chair
- Gloss spray varnish
- White spray paint
- Blending gel
- Sea sponge

8. The book is Bluegrass shaded with Deep Teal and has Lt. Buttermilk pages.

9. **Humpty Dumpty:** Paint the box Cashmere Beige and shade with Cocoa.

10. Paint the egg White and shade with Grey Sky.

11. His suit is Violet Haze shaded with Dioxazine Purple and highlighted with Wisteria.

12. The tie is also Wisteria.

13. The cuffs and collar are White and the shoes are Black.

14. His hands are Base Flesh shaded with Shading Flesh.

15. His features and cracks are Black.

16. **Dish & Spoon:** Paint the dish White and shade with Grey Sky.

Panda
Chair

5. Float White over the tops of the paws, feet, inside the ears, etc., as in the photo.

6. Wash these floats with Black.

7. The eyes have White floats across the top and thin lines across the bottom made with the liner brush.

8. Place White comma strokes in each eye and one on the nose.

9. Apply the pattern to the chair seat and basecoat the bamboo Cashmere Beige.

10. Paint the bamboo leaves Hauser Lt. Green and shade with Hauser Dk. Green.

11. Basecoat the large leaves Hauser Dk. Green and paint the veins Hauser Med. Green.

12. Paint the grass blades Hauser Lt. Green.

13. Paint the pandas the same as the first one.

14. Float Payne's Grey across the bottom of the large bear and under the baby bear's bottom.

15. Float Payne's Grey around the baby bear to make him stand out from the mother bear.

Finishing
1. Finish with several light coats of spray varnish.

2. Attach the single bear to the back of the chair.

1

2

25

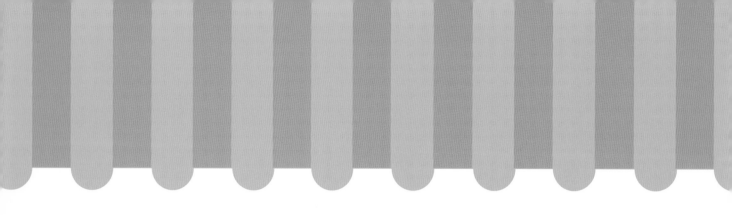

Palette—DecoArt
- Black
- Neutral Grey
- Primary Yellow
- True Red
- White

Brushes—Loew-Cornell
- Series 7000 #4 round
- Series 7300 #12 flat
- Series 7350 10/0 liner
- Series 7550 ¾" wash

Supplies
- Thrift store child's chair
- Sandpaper
- Red spray paint
- ¼" Masonite® or plywood
- Craft saw
- Staple gun
- Gloss spray varnish

Preparation
1. Make any needed repairs and spray paint the chair red.

2. Apply the pattern to the Masonite® and cut out the dog.

3. Sand the edges.

Painting the Design
1. Use the wash brush to basecoat the puppy White.

2. When dry, apply the pattern and use the round brush and Black to paint the eyes.

3. Use the flat brush and Primary Yellow to float a "C" stroke on the eyes

4. Use the liner brush to apply a White comma stroke to each eye for highlight.

5. Use the flat brush to fill in the larger Black areas.

6. Use the liner brush for the smaller areas and to fine tune the stray hairs, such as those that cross the eyes.

7. Use the round brush and True Red for the collar.

8. Use the same brush and Neutral Grey for the dog tag.

Finishing
Spray with several light coats of gloss varnish, allowing the paint to dry between coats.

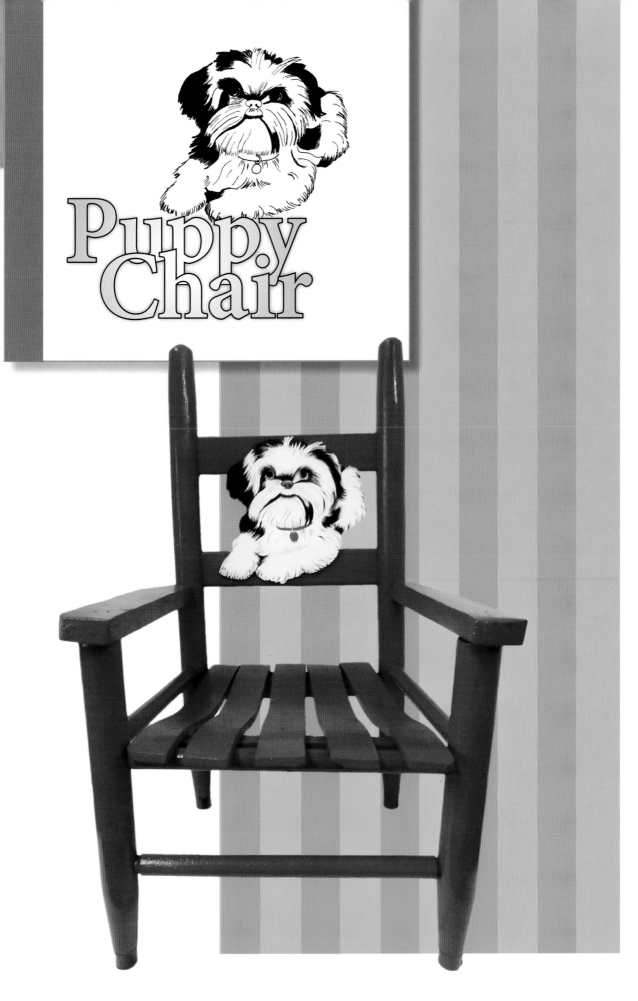

Puppy Chair

Palette—DecoArt
- Black
- Black Plum
- Coral Blush
- Country Blue
- Med. Flesh
- Neutral Grey
- Sapphire Blue
- Shading Flesh
- Slate Grey
- True Red
- White
- Winter Blue

Brushes—Loew-Cornell
- Series 7000 #6 round
- Series 7300 #12 flat
- Series 7350 10/0 liner
- Series 7550 1" wash
- #275 ½" mop

Supplies
- ¼" Masonite®
- Thrift store child's chair
- Sandpaper
- Craft saw
- Red spray paint
- Gloss spray varnish
- Staple gun
- Blending gel
- White spray paint

Preparation
1. Make any needed repairs to the chair.

2. Spray paint it red.

3. Apply the pattern outline to the Masonite® and cut out.

4. Sand any rough edges.

Painting the Design
1. Basecoat the entire cut-out White using the wash brush.

2. Apply the pattern.

Painting Ann:
1. Basecoat her blouse Country Blue and shade with Sapphire Blue.

2. Highlight with Winter Blue.

3. Shade the apron and bloomers with Slate Grey.

4. Paint True Red stripes on the stockings and apron.

5. The shoes and eyes are Black highlighted with Slate Grey.

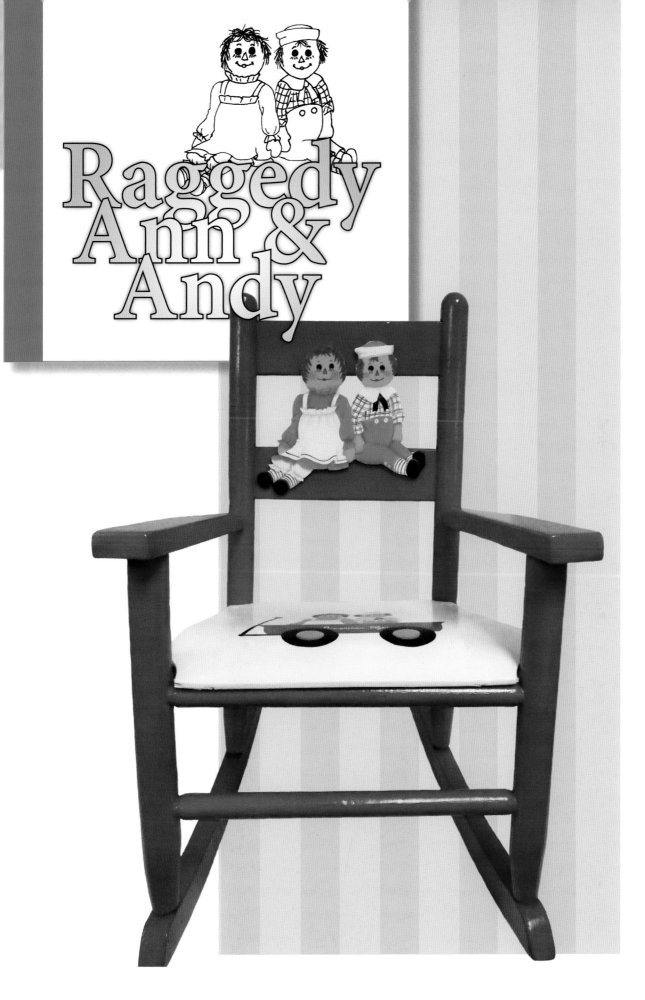

Raggedy Ann & Andy

6. Paint the face and hands with Med. Flesh and shade with Shading Flesh.

7. The hair is True Red shaded with Black Plum.

8. The nose and mouth are also True Red.

9. Use the liner brush to paint the lashes, eyebrows, and mouth line Black.

10. Apply blending gel to the cheeks and touch with Coral Blush; mop to soften.

Painting Andy:
Paint Andy the same way as Ann.

1. His pants and the top of his hat are Country Blue shaded with Sapphire Blue.

2. His shirt is White with Sapphire Blue and True Red lines.

3. The buttons on the pants are White with True Blue dots.

4. His tie is Black highlighted with Slate Grey.

5. The face, hair, and shoes are the same as Ann's.

Wagon
1. Basecoat the wagon True Red.

2. Shade with Black Plum.

3. Paint the wheels and tongue Black.

4. Highlight the wheels with Neutral Grey.

5. Paint the hubcaps Slate Grey and shade with Neutral Grey.

6. Highlight with White.

7. Use White for the lettering.

Finishing
1. Finish with several light coats of spray varnish.

2. Use the staple gun to attach the piece to the back of the chair.

34

Palette—DecoArt
- Black
- Burnt Umber
- Buttermilk
- Flesh Tone
- Honey
- Mink
- Neutral Grey
- Raw Sienna
- Sable
- Slate Grey
- True Ochre
- White

Brushes—Loew-Cornell
- Series 7300 # 12 flat
- Series 7350 10/0 liner
- Series 7520 ½" filbert rake
- Series 7550 1" wash brush
- #275 ½" mop

Supplies
- Thrift store child's chair
- White spray paint
- Gloss spray varnish
- ³/₈" Masonite®
- Craft saw
- Sandpaper
- Blending gel

Preparation
1. Make any needed repairs and spray paint the chair white.

2. Apply the giraffe pattern to the Masonite® and cut out.

3. Sand any rough edges.

1   2   3

Wild
Animals
Chair

Painting the Design
Giraffe:
1. Basecoat the giraffe Buttermilk.

2. Apply the pattern and shade with Raw Sienna.

3. Deepen some shadows with Burnt Umber.

4. Paint the eyes and lashes Black.

5. Paint the stripes on the face and the spots on the neck with Raw Sienna.

6. Apply blending gel to the nose and touch in White. Mop to soften and blend.

7. Use the liner brush and White to add hairs inside the ears.

Seat:
1. Apply the pattern to the seat and basecoat the **antelope** Black, as in the photo.

2. Shade with Slate Grey.

3. Paint the belly White.

4. Basecoat the **tiger** with True Ochre.

5. Shade with Honey.

6. The nose is Flesh Tone.

7. The belly is White; use the filbert rake where the edge meets the True Ochre.

8. Use the filbert rake to paint Black stripes.

9. Paint the **giraffe** the same as the giraffe on the back.

10. Basecoat the **elephant** with a 2:1 mix of Neutral Grey and White.

11. Shade the elephant with Black using a light hand.

12. Basecoat the **monkey** with Sable.

13. Shade the monkey with Burnt Umber and highlight with Mink.

Finishing

1. Finish with several light coats of spray varnish.

2. Fasten the giraffe to the back of the chair.

Christmas Rocking Horse

Palette—DecoArt
- Black
- Black Plum
- Citron
- Country Blue
- Emperor's Gold
- Grey Sky
- Hauser Lt. Green
- Hauser Dk. Green
- Honey
- Neutral Grey
- Pineapple
- Primary Yellow
- Raw Umber
- Sapphire Blue
- Tangerine
- Terra Cotta
- True Ochre
- Tuscan Red
- White
- Winter Blue

Brushes—Loew-Cornell
- Series 7000 #3 round
- Series 7300 #4, 12 flat
- Series 7350 10/0 liner
- Series 7500 #8 filbert rake

Supplies
- Rust-Oleum® Hunter Green spray paint
- Rust-Oleum® Sand spray paint
- Rust-Oleum® White spray paint
- White yarn
- Rocking horse

Preparation
Disassemble the horse, if possible. Spray paint the head and legs Sand, the rockers, handles, and crosspieces Hunter Green, and the seat White.

Painting the design:
1. Apply the pattern to the head and basecoat the candy canes White.

2. Paint the stripes Tuscan Red.

3. Shade the white edges Winter Blue.

4. Shade the red edges Black Plum.

5. Shade under the candy Terra Cotta.

6. Apply the pattern to the seat and paint the red sections Tuscan Red.

7. Shade the same way you did the mane.

8. Add a thin White line in a circle for shine.

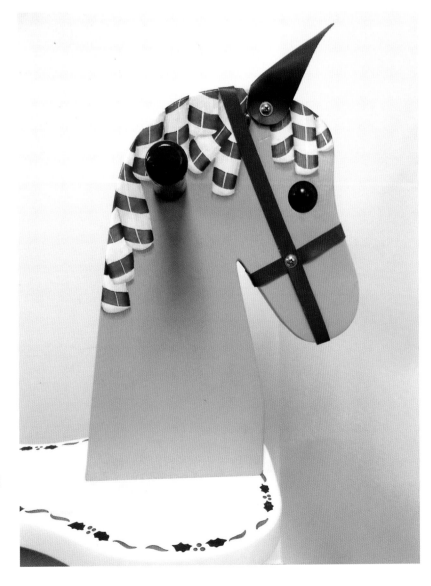

43

9. Paint the holly Hauser Dk. Green.

10. Use a stylus to make the Tuscan Red holly berries.

11. Apply the pattern and basecoat the bells on the crosspieces Honey.

12. Repaint using Emperor's Gold.

13. Use the #12 brush to shade the bells with Burnt Umber.

14. Use the liner brush and Black for the holes.

15. Paint the ribbon White and shade with Winter Blue.

16. Use the stylus to make the dots along the edges of the ribbon.

17. Apply the pattern on the legs and use the liner brush to paint the wires on the string of bulbs Black.

18. Use the #4 flat brush to paint the bulb sockets Grey Sky.

19. Shade the bulb sockets with Neutral Grey.

20. Using the #8 filbert brush, paint the red bulbs Tuscan Red.

21. Using the #12 flat brush, shade with Black Plum.

22. Highlight with Tangerine.

23. Paint the yellow bulbs Primary Yellow.

24. Shade with True Ochre.

25. Highlight with Pineapple.

26. Paint the blue bulbs Country Blue.

27. Shade with Sapphire Blue.

28. Highlight with Winter Blue.

29. Paint the green bulbs Hauser Lt. Green.

30. Shade with Hauser Dk. Green.

31. Highlight with Citron.

32. Shade under all the bulbs with Terra Cotta.

Finishing
1. Spray with several light coats of varnish.

2. Measure out 40 strands of yarn 24" long.

3. Tie in the middle and cut the loops.

4. When varnish is dry, staple the tail in place.

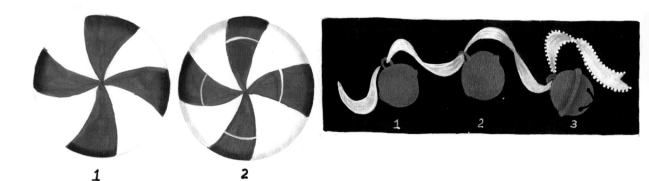

1   2

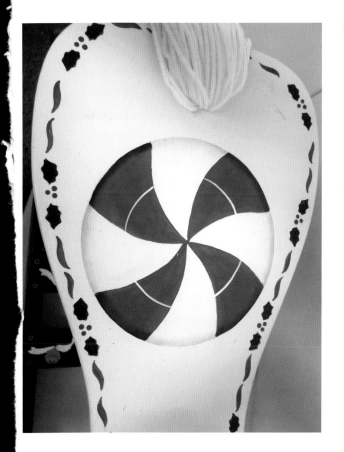

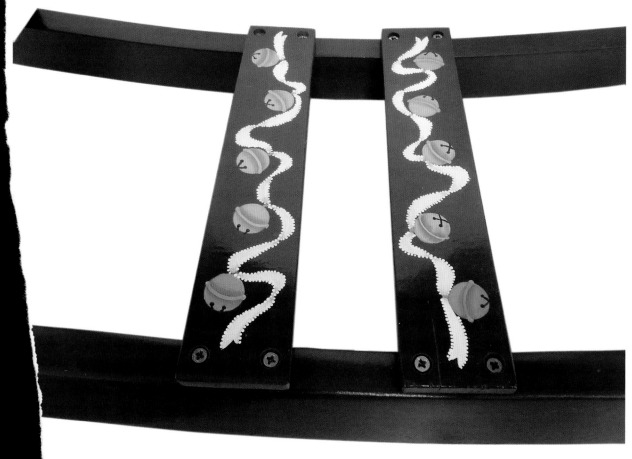

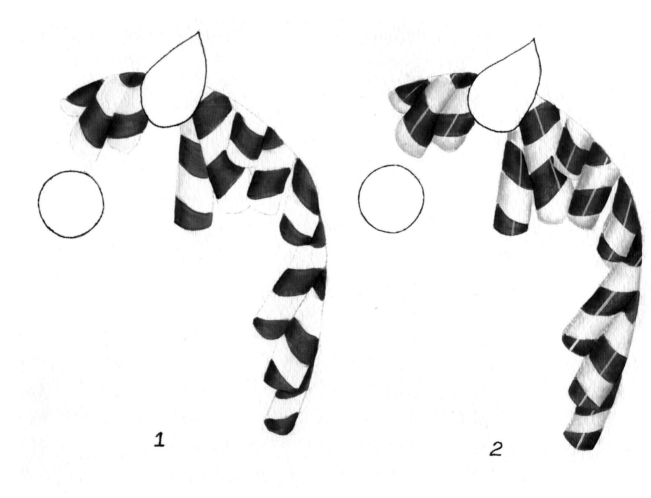

1

2

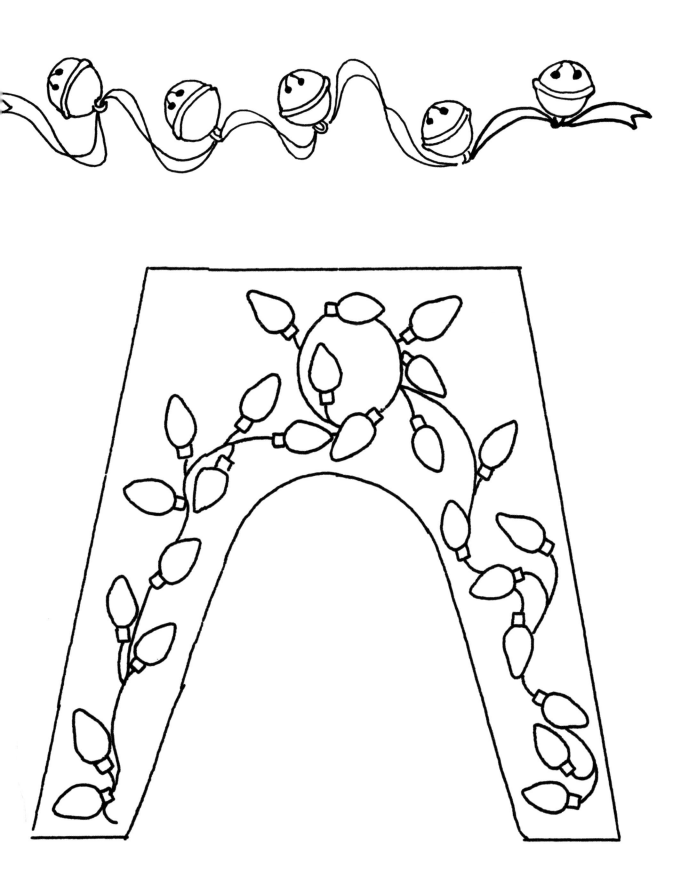

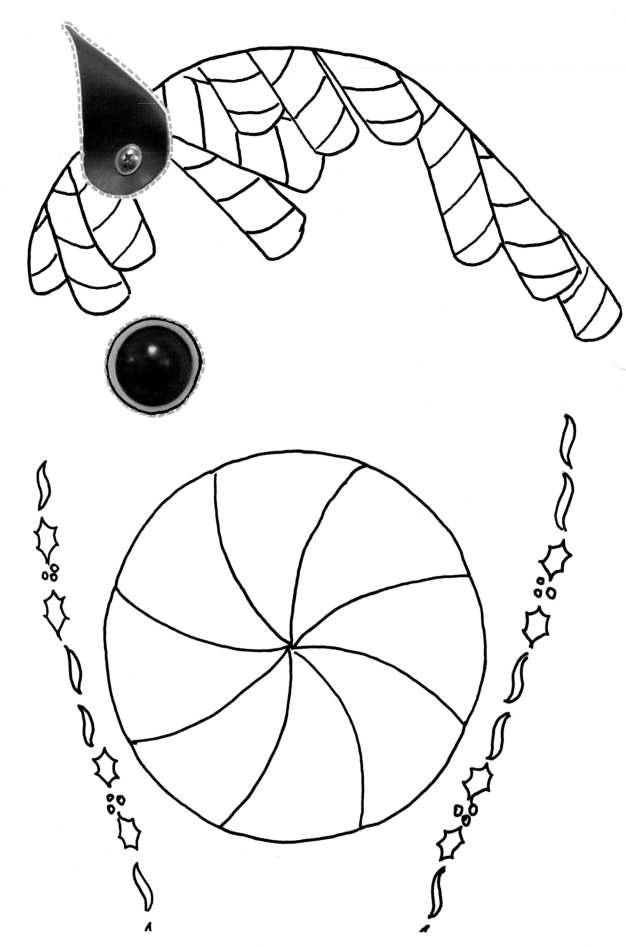